Lincoln Township Public Library
2099 W. John Beers Rd.
Stevensville, MI 49127

W9-BAI-720

HORSEPOWER

DIRT BIKES

by Matt Doeden

Reading Consultant:

Barbara J. Fox

Reading Specialist

North Carolina State University

Capstone press

Mankato, Minnesota

Blazers is published by Capstone Press
151 Good Counsel Drive, P.O. Box 669, Mankato, Minnesota 56002
www.capstonepress.com

Copyright © 2005 by Capstone Press. All rights reserved.
No part of this publication may be reproduced in whole or in part, or stored in a retrieval
system, or transmitted in any form or by any means, electronic, mechanical,
photocopying, recording, or otherwise, without written permission of the publisher.
For information regarding permission, write to Capstone Press,
151 Good Counsel Drive, P.O. Box 669, Dept. R, Mankato, Minnesota 56002.
Printed in the United States of America

Library of Congress Cataloging-in-Publication Data
Doeden, Matt.
    Dirt bikes / by Matt Doeden.
    p. cm.—(Blazers. horsepower)
    Includes bibliographical references and index.
    ISBN 0-7368-2733-1 (hardcover)
    1. Trail bikes—Juvenile literature. [1. Trail bikes. 2.
    Motorcycling.]
    I. Title. II. Series: Horsepower (Mankato, Minn.)
TL441.D64 2005
629.227'5—dc22   2003026085

Summary: Discusses dirt bikes, their main features, and how
    they are raced.

Editorial Credits
James Anderson, editor; Jason Knudson, designer; Jo Miller,
    photo researcher; Eric Kudalis, product planning editor

Photo Credits
Corbis/NewSport/Larry Lasperek, 18–19; Tom Stewart, 12–13
Getty Images/Gary Newkirk, 22; Mike Hewitt, 28–29
Kinney Jones Photography, 21, 27 (both)
Steve Bruhn, cover, 5 (both), 6, 7, 8, 9, 14–15, 16, 17, 23, 24, 25
X-Gen Photo/Anthony Scavo, 10–11, 26

The publisher does not endorse products whose logos may appear on objects
in images in this book.

1 2 3 4 5 6 09 08 07 06 05 04

TABLE OF CONTENTS

Lincoln Township Public Library
2099 W. John Beers Rd.
Stevensville, MI 49127
(269) 429-9575

THE BIG FINISH

Dirt bike riders steer their bikes around the final turns. The engines whine. The rider on bike number 18 takes the lead.

The riders speed up after the turns. Number 18 still has the lead. The riders on bikes 52 and 259 battle for second place.

The rider on the number 52 bike cranks his throttle and gains on number 259. Number 18 wins. Number 52 is close behind.

BLAZER FACT

Some dirt bike riders practice on mountain bikes to get to know the track.

DIRT BIKE TRACTION

Dirt bikes are lightweight.
They handle well on dirt, mud,
and sand.

Dirt bike tires have deep
tread. Bumps and grooves allow
the tires to grip the dirt better.

BLAZER FACT

Riders use different tires for different tracks. They use tires with deeper tread for loose dirt or mud.

DIRT BIKE SPEED

Dirt bike racers quickly gain speed. They go fast enough to land safely after 80-foot (24-meter) jumps.

Riders use controls on the handlebars. The throttle and brake change the bike's speed.

BLAZER FACT

Riders as young as
four years old race
small dirt bikes.

DIRT BIKE DIAGRAM

Exhaust

Tire

Handlebars

Shock Absorbers

Engine

DIRT BIKES IN ACTION

Riders race in motocross and supercross events. Motocross races take place outdoors. Supercross races are indoors.

Jeremy McGrath was the first dirt bike racing star. He was a supercross champion seven times.

BLAZER FACT

Jeremy McGrath first raced
BMX bikes when he was
10 years old. At 14, he
switched to dirt bikes.

Freestyle is the newest dirt bike event. Riders do backflips, spins, and grabs off huge ramps.

BLAZER FACT

Mike Metzger and Travis Pastrana were the first riders to do backflips in competitions.

Ricky Carmichael is one of the best dirt bike racers. In 2002, he won his fourth motocross championship.

DIRT BIKE RACERS SPEED THROUGH MUD!

GLOSSARY

handlebars (HAN-duhl-barz)—the bars at the front of a dirt bike that are used for steering

lightweight (LITE-wayt)—not heavy

motocross (MOH-toh-kross)—a sport in which dirt bikes race on an outdoor track

supercross (SOO-puhr-kross)—a dirt bike race that takes place on an indoor track

throttle (THROT-uhl)—a grip on the handlebar that controls how much fuel and air flow into a dirt bike engine

READ MORE

Blomquist, Christopher. *Motocross in the X Games.* A Kid's Guide to the X Games. New York: PowerKids Press, 2003.

Parr, Danny. *Dirt Bikes.* Wild Rides! Mankato, Minn.: Capstone Press, 2002.

Schaefer, A. R. *Extreme Freestyle Motocross Moves.* Behind the Moves. Mankato, Minn.: Capstone Press, 2003.

INTERNET SITES

FactHound offers a safe, fun way to find Internet sites related to this book. All of the sites on FactHound have been researched by our staff.

Here's how:

1. Visit *www.facthound.com*
2. Type in this special code **0736827331** for age-appropriate sites. Or, enter a search word related to this book for a more general search.
3. Click on the **Fetch It** button.

FactHound will fetch the best sites for you!

INDEX

Lincoln Township Public Library
2099 W. John Beers Rd.
Stevensville, MI 49127
(269) 429-9575